PeAks and valleys

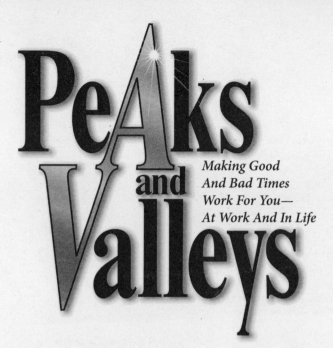

PeAks and Valleys

Making Good
And Bad Times
Work For You—
At Work And In Life

Spencer Johnson, M.D.

**SIMON &
SCHUSTER**

London · New York · Sydney · Toronto · New Delhi

A CBS COMPANY

First published in Great Britain by Simon & Schuster UK Ltd, 2009
This paperback edition published by Simon & Schuster UK Ltd, 2014
A CBS COMPANY

First published in the US in 2009 by Atria Books,
A division of Simon & Schuster, Inc.
1230 Avenue of the Americas
New York, NY 10020

Designed by Nancy Singer

3 5 7 9 10 8 6 4 2

Simon & Schuster UK Ltd
1st Floor
222 Gray's Inn Road
London WC1X 8HB

www.simonandschuster.co.uk

Simon & Schuster Australia, Sydney
Simon & Schuster India, New Delhi

A CIP catalogue record for this book
is available from the British Library.

Paperback ISBN: 978-1-84739-648-8
Ebook ISBN: 978-1-45160-661-4

Printed and bound by CPI Group (UK) Ltd, Croydon, CR0 4YY

The real voyage of discovery consists not in seeing new landscapes, but in having new eyes.

—Proust

Bad things happen because of what we did in good times.

Good things happen because of what we did in bad times.

—Roberto C. Goizueta, Former CEO
The Coca-Cola Company

The essence of knowledge is, having it, to use it.

—Confucius

Contents

Before The Story

Early one rainy evening in New York, Michael Brown hurried to meet someone a friend had said might help him deal with a difficult time he was having. As he entered the small café, he had no way of knowing how valuable the next few hours would be.

When he saw Ann Carr, he was surprised. He had heard she had been through some tough times herself and expected it to show on her. But she seemed upbeat and full of energy.

After some preliminary conversation, he said, "You look like you're in a good place, despite the bad times I understand you've been through."

She said, "I *am* in a good place, both in my work and in my life. But it's not *in spite* of the bad times. It's *because* of them—and how I learned to take advantage of them."

Michael was puzzled. "How so?" he asked.

"Well, for example, at work I thought our department was doing fine, but in reality we weren't. We'd been successful, but we'd become complacent. By the time we realized it, other companies were doing much better than we were. My boss became very unhappy with me.

"That's when I started feeling low, and the pressure to improve things in a hurry began. Each day became more stressful."

Michael asked, "So, what happened?"

She answered, "I heard a story last year from someone at work I respected. It changed how I looked at good and bad times, and what I do now is very different. The story helped me to be calmer and more successful, whether things are going well or not, even in my personal life. I'll never forget it!"

"What was the story?" he asked.

Ann was quiet for a moment, and then said, "Would it be all right if I asked why you would like to know about it?"

Michael reluctantly admitted that he was not feeling very secure in his job, and things were not going so well for him at home.

He didn't need to say any more. She felt his embarrassment, and said, "You sound like you need to hear the story as much as I did."

Ann said she would tell Michael the story with the understanding that if he found it valuable, he would share it with others. He agreed, and Ann prepared Michael for what he was about to hear.

She said, "I found that if you want to use the story to deal with the ups and downs that come at you, it helps if you listen with your heart and head, and fill in the story with your own experience to see what is true for *you*.

"The insights in the story are often repeated, although in slightly different ways."

Michael asked "Why the repetition?"

She answered, "Well, for me, it made it easier to remember them. And when I remembered the insights, I used them more."

She admitted, "I'm reluctant to change. So, I need to hear something new often enough that, at some point, it gets past my critical, distrusting mind, becomes more familiar, and touches my heart. Then it becomes a part of me.

"That's what happened after I thought a lot about the story. But you can discover that for yourself, if you like."

"Do you really think a story can make that big a difference?" Michael asked. "I'm in a pretty tough spot right now."

Ann replied, "In that case, what do you have to lose? All I can tell you is that when I applied what I got out of the story, it had a big impact.

"Some people," she cautioned, "get very little from the story, while others get a great deal!

"It's not the story; it's what you take away from it that is so powerful. That's up to you, of course."

Michael nodded. "Okay. I think I would really like to hear it."

So Ann started to tell the tale over dinner, and then continued through dessert and coffee.

She began:

The Story of

Peaks and Valleys

1

Feeling Low In A Valley

Once there was a bright young man who lived unhappily in a valley, until he went to see an old man who lived on a peak.

When he was younger, he had been happy in his valley. He played in its meadows and swam in its river.

The valley was all he had ever known, and he thought he would spend his whole life there.

Some days in his valley were cloudy and some were sunny, but there was a sameness to his daily routine that he found comforting.

However, as he grew older, he began to see what was wrong more often than he noticed what was right. He wondered why he had not noticed before how many things were wrong in the valley.

As time went on, the young man became increasingly unhappy, although he wasn't sure why.

He tried working at different jobs in the valley, but none turned out to be what he had hoped for.

In one job, his boss always seemed to criticize him for what he did wrong and never noticed all the things he did right.

In another, he was one of so many employees that it didn't seem to matter to anyone whether he worked hard or hardly worked at all. His contribution seemed invisible, even to himself.

Once, he thought he had finally found what he wanted. He felt appreciated and challenged, he worked with capable colleagues, and he was proud of the company's product. He worked his way up and became manager of a small department.

Unfortunately, he felt his job was not secure.

His personal life was no better. One disappointment seemed to follow another.

He thought his friends didn't understand, and his family told him he was "just going through a phase."

The young man wondered if he would be better off someplace else.

Sometimes the young man would stand in the meadow and look up at the range of majestic peaks that rose high above his valley.

He would imagine himself standing on the nearby peak.

For a while, he felt better.

But the more he compared the peak to his valley, the worse he felt.

He spoke to his parents and friends about going to the peak. But they talked only about how difficult it was to reach the peak, and how comfortable it was to stay in the valley.

They all discouraged him from going where they themselves had never been.

The young man loved his parents and knew there was some truth to what they said. But he also knew that he was a different person from his father and mother.

Sometimes he felt there might be a different way of life outside the valley, and he wanted to discover it for himself. Maybe on the peak he could gain a better view of the world.

But then doubt and fear crept in again, and he thought he would stay where he was.

For a long time the young man could not bring himself to leave his valley.

Then one day, he recalled his early youth and realized how much had changed since then. He was no longer at peace with himself.

He wasn't sure why he changed his mind, but he suddenly decided he had to go visit that mountaintop.

He put his fear aside and got ready to leave as quickly as he could. Then, he set out for the nearby peak.

It was not an easy journey. It took him much longer than he thought it would to make it less than halfway up the peak.

But as the young man went higher, the cool breeze and fresh air revitalized him. From higher up, his valley looked smaller.

When he had been down in the valley, the air seemed clean enough. But when he viewed the valley from above, he saw the pale brown stagnant air that was trapped there.

Then he turned and continued upward. The higher he climbed, the more he could see.

Suddenly, the trail he was following ended.

With no trail to follow, he became lost among the thick trees that blocked out the light. He feared he would not find his way out.

So, he decided to cross a dangerously narrow ridge. As he did, he fell. Bruised and bleeding, he picked himself up and continued on.

Eventually, he found a new path.

The warnings of the people in the valley crossed his mind. But then he gathered his courage and kept climbing.

The higher he went, the happier he became, knowing that he was leaving the valley and putting aside his fears.

He was on his way to someplace new.

As he rose above the clouds, he realized it was a beautiful day and imagined how the sunset would look from the summit. He could hardly wait to see it from up there.

2

Finding Answers

Despite the young man's eagerness, he did not reach the peak until nightfall. He sat down and groaned, "Oh, no! Missed it!"

A voice nearby in the darkness asked, "Missed what?"

Startled, the young man turned and saw an old man sitting on a large boulder a few feet away.

The young man stammered, "Sorry, I didn't see you there. I missed seeing the sunset from the peak. I'm afraid that's the story of my life."

The old man laughed and said, "I know the feeling."

At that moment, the young man had no way of knowing that he had just met one of the most peaceful and successful people in the world. He just seemed like a nice old man.

After a while, the old man said, "So, what do you think of the view now?"

"What view?" the young man asked. He squinted into the darkness but could see no view. He was beginning to wonder about his new acquaintance.

The old man leaned back and looked up at the sky.

In turn, the young man also looked up and saw an array of stars sparkling overhead. He had never seen the stars so clearly from his valley.

"Beautiful, isn't it?" the old man said.

"Yes!" the young man said in amazement. Gazing at the stars, he enjoyed a peaceful moment. "They were there all the time, weren't they?"

"Well, yes. And no," the old man said. "Yes, they were there all the time. You just needed to change what you were looking at."

Then he added, "And no. Not really. Scientists say that much of the light we are looking at now was sent millions of years ago from fading stars that are no longer there."

The young man shook his head and said, "It's hard to know what's real and what's not."

The old man said nothing. He just smiled.

When the young man asked what he was smiling about, the old man replied, "I was just thinking of how often I felt the same way at your age. Trying to sort out fact from fiction."

For a time they sat in silence, marveling at the light show taking place above them.

Then the old man asked, "Why have you come up to the peak?"

"I'm not sure," the young man admitted. "I guess I'm looking for something."

He began telling the old man how unhappy he was down in his valley, and how he felt there had to be a better way.

He told him about the jobs he had tried, the relationships that didn't seem to work, and the sense that he wasn't living up to his potential.

He was surprised to hear himself revealing so much to a total stranger.

The old man listened closely. After the young man had finished, the old man said, "I remember being down many times myself.

"I can still remember being fired from my first job. It was terrible. As hard as I tried, I couldn't find any work."

"So what did you do?"

"Well, for too long, I just got angry and depressed. Things didn't go well for me. But then a good friend of mine, someone I will never forget, told me something that changed everything."

"What was that?" the young man asked.

"It was about what he called *the Peaks and Valleys approach to good and bad times.*

"He said, 'The more you use a Peaks and Valleys approach in your work and personal life, the more peaceful and successful you become.'"

The old man added, "I was pretty skeptical at first, but it turned out to be true. And it had a huge impact on my career and my life."

"How so?" the young man wanted to know.

"It changed how I looked at the ups and downs in my life. And thanks to that, I changed what I *did*."

The young man asked, "In what way?"

"My friend helped me discover three things: how to get out of a Valley sooner; how to stay on a Peak longer; and how to have more Peaks and fewer Valleys in my future."

The young man wondered if it was too good to be true. But he was here looking for answers and he was curious, so he asked, "Will you tell me about it?"

The old man said, "I will, on the condition that if you find it useful, you will share it with others."

"Why share it with others?" the young man said.

The old man answered, "There are two reasons: first, to help them; and second, to help yourself.

"When people around you know how to make both good and bad times work for them, they worry less and do better. And that makes working and living with them more enjoyable for you."

The young man said that if it worked for him, he would indeed share it with others.

Then the old man began, "It may be useful to start with this:

*It Is Natural For
Everyone Everywhere To
Have Peaks And Valleys
At Work And In Life.*

The young man was disappointed. This wasn't the answer he was hoping for.

"What exactly do you mean by 'peaks and valleys'?" he asked.

"I mean your *personal* Peaks and Valleys—the highs and lows you feel at work and in life.

"These good or bad moments may last for minutes, or for months, or longer.

"Personal Peaks and Valleys are as natural as the physical peaks and valleys you see on the earth's surface. Both kinds of highs and lows are scattered about and connected in similar ways.

"You can feel up in one area of your work or life, and down in another. It's natural. It happens to everyone in the world, in every culture. It is part of being human."

The young man sighed and said, "So I'm not the only one."

The old man laughed. "Not even close! Though sometimes you might feel like it."

He added, "There is obviously great variety in the up and down moments we each have, because no two people's experiences are exactly alike, even when we're in similar situations.

"You might think of it like this:

Peaks And Valleys
Are Not Just The
Good And Bad Times
That Happen To You.

They Are Also
How You Feel Inside
And Respond To
Outside Events.

"How you feel depends largely on how you view your situation. The key is to separate what happens to you from how good and valuable you feel you are as a person."

The old man continued, "I found that you can feel good about yourself even when bad things are happening to—"

Suddenly, the young man interrupted him.

"So you're saying that when things down in the valley weren't working out for me, I somehow should have been happy? Hate to disagree with you, sir, but I do.

"*Nothing* was working out for me down there! It's easy for you to say all this, sitting up here on this peak. Your life up here doesn't have anything to do with my life down in the valley! It's a whole other world where I come from."

The old man did not seem offended by the young man's outburst. He just stayed quiet.

After a time, the young man grew calmer. He became embarrassed and said, "I'm sorry. I knew I was discouraged, but I guess I'm also a little angry—more than I realized."

The old man nodded. "I understand."

Then he said, "So, you think my life up here has no connection with your life down in the valley. Let me ask you something.

"Did you notice a gap on your way up here—a large hole in the ground that separated your valley from this peak?"

"No, I didn't," said the young man. "Where was it?"

The old man said nothing.

The young man thought, and then laughed. "That's because there wasn't one, was there."

"Very good," the old man said.

"Because peaks and valleys are connected," the young man said.

"How observant," the old man said with a smile. "Who is to say where the highest part of the valley ends and the lowest part of the peak begins?

"The key is to understand not only that both physical peaks and valleys, and personal Peaks and Valleys are connected, but also *how* they are connected."

Then he expanded on what he had said:

Peaks And Valleys Are Connected.

The Errors You Make In
Today's Good Times
Create Tomorrow's Bad Times.

And The Wise Things You Do In
Today's Bad Times
Create Tomorrow's Good Times.

"For example, people who use a Peaks and Valleys approach during bad times make things better when they return to basics, and concentrate on what matters most."

The young man added, ". . . which is what creates good times for them later!"

"Yes," the old man said. "But then too many people fail to manage their good times and do not notice that they are creating their own future bad times. They waste too many resources, get away from the basics, and ignore what matters most. And guess what happens?"

The young man said, "Bad times again!"

The young man had to admit this made sense. "So we actually *create* our own good and bad times, far more than we realize."

"Exactly!" the old man exclaimed. His eyes brightened as he observed the young man starting to make his own discoveries.

"Perhaps that's enough to think about for one night," the old man said. "If you like, we can talk tomorrow."

"I would like that very much."

Then the old man said good night and left the young man to set up his tent and make camp.

Later, the young man fell asleep thinking about how his own personal Peaks and Valleys might be connected.

Early the next morning, the old man arrived carrying a thermos of hot coffee to share.

In the bright morning light, the young man noticed how clear the old man's eyes were, and said, "You seem happy. Is that because you always get to stay up here on this peak?"

"No, that's not why I'm happy. And I don't always get to stay here. I have to go into the valley to get supplies and find what I need to live here."

The young man was still sleepy and did not really grasp what the old man was saying. "I think I could be happy up here forever," he responded.

"But you cannot," said the old man. "No one can stay in one place forever. Even if you remain physically in one spot, you are always moving in and out of the places in your heart.

"The secret is to *truly* appreciate and enjoy each time for what it is while you are living it."

"I don't know about that," the young man said. "All I know is, I am enjoying life just fine up here on this peak in this crisp, clean air.

"But how am I supposed to enjoy the time I spend in a Valley?"

"Actually," the old man said, "how you experience a Valley has a lot to do with how long you'll remain in it. A useful way to think of Peaks and Valleys is this:

Peaks Are Moments When
You Appreciate What You Have.

Valleys Are Moments When
You Long For What Is Missing.

"Interesting," the young man said. "But it seems to me that a Peak is a Peak, no matter what I think about it, and a Valley is a Valley. What do my thoughts have to do with it?"

The old man asked, "Do you remember the first thing you said, when you arrived on this peak?"

The young man tried, but couldn't remember.

"You said, 'Missed it.' You focused on missing the sunset and did not see the stars. You did not even celebrate making it to the peak.

"How do you think you would have felt when you arrived up here if you'd raised your arms over your head and shouted, 'Yes! I made it!'?"

The young man sighed. "So, I changed my personal Peak into a Valley. I'd made it all the way here to the place I'd dreamed of for years, but I still felt like I'd failed."

The old man said, "Yes. Do you see, in that moment, you created a Valley in your own mind?"

Then the old man asked, "How could someone win a Silver Medal for outstanding performance and be unhappy?"

The young man thought about it and said, "By comparing it to winning a Gold Medal." Then he realized, "So, if you want to have fewer Valleys, avoid comparisons. If you enjoy what's good about the moment, you feel more like you are on a Peak."

"Yes!" the old man said, "even in bad times.

"What if you realized this instead:

You Cannot Always
Control External Events,

But You Can Control
Your Personal
Peaks And Valleys
By What You Believe
And What You Do.

The young man frowned. "I'm not sure I understand. How would I do this? You said it would help me at work and in life."

"So I did. To change a Valley into a Peak, you need to change one of two things: what is happening, or how you *feel* about what is happening.

"If you can change the situation, that's great. If not, you can choose how you feel about it so that it can work to your advantage."

"How?" the young man asked.

"For example, imagine that you are the sole financial support for your family and you have what you believe is a secure, well-paying job. Without warning, you learn that you have been fired—and you see no real chance for immediate employment. How do you feel?"

"Frightened. Stunned. Angry."

"Understandable. That is how most people would feel. But what if you saw that leaving your job, although you didn't like getting fired, was one of the best things that ever happened to you?

"What if you realized later on that you and the job might not have been well suited for each other, and while you might never have chosen to leave at that moment, it may have been something you should have done long ago?

"What if you chose to believe that getting fired could result in something better?"

The young man said, "But it could lead to something worse."

The old man laughed. "That's true. No one knows what's going to happen.

"However, in reality, choosing a better belief usually leads you to a much better result."

The still-skeptical young man asked, "But how is that practical for the person who is now out of work? They may feel better about the situation— but they still need a job. You can't feed a family on good feelings."

The old man said, "Fair enough. Okay, let's be *truly* practical. If you were the one hiring a new employee, who would you be more likely to hire— someone who looked downtrodden and spent the interview complaining about how badly their former employer treated them?

Or the person who looked for the good in the bad time, and felt free to pursue a new opportunity and find something better?"

The young man said, "The positive person, because they're more likely to do a better job."

The old man said, "And that's why the person with the better belief usually gets a better job. So, what happened to that person's Valley?"

The young man was amazed. "It changed into a Peak! So what the person *believed* and *did* actually made a difference. Maybe this really *is* practical!"

"Yes. It's very practical," the old man said. "Sometimes it's as simple as this:

*The Path Out Of
The Valley Appears
When You Choose To
See Things Differently.*

By this time, the temperature on the mountaintop had dropped, and a few snowflakes had begun to fall. The old man asked, "Are you prepared to stay on the peak?"

The young man admitted he had not brought warm clothes. "I guess I was in such a hurry to get out of the valley, I wasn't really thinking about what I'd need to stay up here."

The old man said, "That's not unusual. Many people don't realize that they need to be *truly* prepared if they want to stay on a Peak longer."

The young man didn't understand that the old man was referring to managing your good times.

"I hope you come back up again," the old man added. "I have enjoyed your visit." With that, he shook the young man's hand and said good-bye.

The young man was disappointed to leave the peak, but encouraged by what he had found there.

He told himself that he would now see his work and life differently. He hoped he would see a Valley as an opportunity to discover the hidden good that makes things better.

He took a deep breath of the fresh mountain air and hoped he would be able to keep his clarity when he was back in his valley.

He made a mental note of what he wanted to remember:

You Change Your
Valley Into A Peak

When You Find And
Use The Good

That Is Hidden
In The Bad Time.

3

Forgetting

When the young man arrived back in his valley, he recalled how he used to stand in the meadow and look up at the distant peak and dream about finding a different way of life up there.

Then he felt a flush of excitement. He had actually ascended the peak! And just as he had hoped, he *had* gained a better view.

Now he was eager to return to his job with his new outlook. He wondered what his parents and friends would think when he told them all about his adventure.

As he headed for home, he thought, "The view from this valley is so much smaller. Viewed from atop the peak, where I've been, it's so much easier to see the big picture."

He was very pleased with himself.

He thought about a special young woman who he cared about, and hoped she would be impressed with his journey and his newfound knowledge.

When he reached his home, he told his parents about his journey up the mountain, and what he had learned from the old man who lived there.

With this new philosophy, he told them, he would become a great asset at work, and would no doubt soon be in line for a promotion.

His parents looked at each other, thinking this sounded boastful, but they said nothing.

The young man, however, was not as sure about all this as he sounded. He wondered if this new outlook would really make such a big difference. Secretly, he still had his doubts, but he was eager to try it out and see.

Soon he proudly told some of his friends about what he'd learned on the peak.

Some were fascinated, while others were skeptical. It sounded so simple, could it really work? But like most good friends, they wanted him to succeed.

He also told the young woman he cared about. She was intrigued with his story, and glad to see how excited he seemed. She hoped his newfound enthusiasm would last.

When he went back to work, he was happy.

Business was good at his company. Sales were increasing, and profits were at an all-time high.

Then one day a very important shipment got lost and no one could find it. Their largest customer was so unhappy that they threatened to cancel their account.

Everyone at work tried frantically to fix the problem. Some worked on making up the shortfall, while others focused on tracking down the missing shipment.

But the company had grown too fast and people were stretched too thin. Despite their efforts, other shipments were also lost. Many customers began canceling orders. The mood at work was bleak.

The young man remembered what the old man had said about getting out of a Valley: *You can change your Valley into a Peak when you find and use the good that is hidden in the bad time.*

That night, he kept thinking about it.

The next day he went to his boss with an idea. What if they used this crisis as an opportunity to find the weaknesses in their order-tracking system, and used what they found to create a better, more reliable system for future orders?

His boss liked the idea and asked him to lead a team to make it happen.

After several days, the team found key flaws in their system that led them to develop a much more reliable and less expensive way of handling orders.

They apologized to their customers who were glad to learn about the better delivery system that was now available and at a lower cost. Many began to reorder—small orders at first, but there was hope that larger orders would soon follow.

Word got around that the new order system had been the work of the bright young man's team. His reputation improved among his coworkers, and his boss was so pleased, he gave him a raise.

Before long, he went to his boss with another suggestion: Why not invest in growing new markets they'd never gone into before?

But his boss said no. He felt they were doing fine as they were. And he reminded the young man that he was still the youngest manager and he had just received a raise. That should satisfy him.

The young man realized that his boss, like many others in the company, was satisfied with things as they were. Many more things began to go wrong, both outside and inside the company, but no one seemed to notice.

Most people in the company continued to act as if they were still in good times. As the business had grown, people had lost track of what made them successful in the first place.

Many departments overspent, confident that the company was doing well.

Larger problems began to plague the company. Income dropped substantially and they had to cut expenses. People were laid off, including some of the young man's friends.

Times were becoming bad.

At least the young man was able to keep his position and was well regarded since he had helped with his team's more efficient order and delivery system.

He had even proudly told his parents how well he was doing at work.

But before long, he got caught up in his own success and became so confident that he stopped listening to anyone but himself.

Over time, he forgot to use much of what he had learned on the peak.

Without realizing it, he began to alienate the people around him. His coworkers started avoiding him, and his boss began criticizing him.

His newfound confidence soon began to fade.

Things at work were clearly going wrong, but he could not figure out why.

When his parents tried to talk with him, he didn't listen. He just defended his behavior, which only made things worse. As time went on, the young man found himself back in a deeper Valley.

Then he recalled a piece of advice the old man gave him before he had returned to his valley:

Between Peaks There
Are Always Valleys.

How You Manage Your Valley
Determines How Soon
You Reach Your Next Peak.

He wondered, "How exactly do you manage a Valley?" If the old man had talked about that, he couldn't recall what he'd said.

He went looking for his friends, but nobody seemed to be around. He did not realize it, of course, but his friends were avoiding him.

He had not heard from the young woman in quite a while and wondered why. "She's probably just busy," he told himself.

Before long, he felt even lonelier than he had been before he'd gone to the peak.

He reminded himself that it is natural to have Peaks and Valleys.

He tried to find the path out of his Valley by choosing to see things differently.

He tried to find the hidden good in the situation and see how he could use it to his advantage.

But nothing made him feel any better.

Initially, the Peaks and Valleys approach had helped him become more successful.

But now it wasn't working, and he couldn't understand why.

He went back to the meadow again and looked up at the mountain.

The Peaks and Valleys approach had sounded good when the old man described it. But here in the real world, it was starting to seem like it was nothing but a fairy tale that was too good to last.

Maybe his doubting friends were right.

He went off to think and rested for a while beside a quiet pond. Looking down, he caught a glimpse of his reflection. He did not like what he saw.

He knew he was becoming more resentful and was not at peace with himself. Then he remembered something else the old man had said:

If you do not learn in a Valley, you can become bitter. If you truly learn something valuable, you can become better.

But if that was true, what was it that he needed to learn?

After many weeks, the young man got tired of trying to figure it all out.

A few of his friends suggested that he join them out on the plateau, where they liked to go and "dull out," as they called it.

He had never been to the plateau, but from what he had heard, it wasn't that hard to get to. It certainly wasn't as far away as the peak.

And being dulled out on the plateau had to be better than feeling low in the valley.

So he set out for the plateau.

4

Resting

The young man was surprised to see how barren it was on the plateau. There were no trees and it was flat as far as the eye could see.

The tepid weather was neither as warm as the valley, nor as cool as the peak. An overcast sky blocked the sun. It was almost as though there was no weather at all.

At times, he saw other people in the distance, but he avoided them. He wanted to be alone.

At first he was relieved to feel little or nothing. He was glad he had come to the plateau.

He soon began to recover from the stress of all the ups and downs he had been feeling. He liked just being where he was. It felt restful.

Later on, he was glad to find his friends, but they did not seem enthusiastic about seeing him.

Their eyes were as flat and lifeless as the surroundings. They did not seem interested in what was going on around them. They did not look healthy or vibrant, even in the outdoors.

The young man looked at his friends, and wondered if he was starting to look like that, too. He was afraid he might be.

The young man became bored and restless. When he had first arrived on the plateau, it was refreshing to take a break from everything.

Now it felt like everything was starting to drain from him. He was not enthusiastic, like he once felt on the peak.

When he had been in the valley, it had seemed like a good idea to go to the plateau.

But now he wondered why he was still here. A plateau, he thought, was a neutral time when you felt neither high nor low.

So what was this plateau for him? Was he just taking a well deserved break, and resting? Or was he here to escape? And if so, what was he escaping from?

And what about his friends? Were they just trying to escape reality by dulling their senses?

Eventually, he said good-bye to the others and went off on his own.

The young man could barely see the peak from where he was. He looked up, and thought about what the old man might be doing now.

He remembered looking into the old man's face and seeing the brightness and clarity in his eyes. A part of him wished he was back there.

The clarity he found on the peak was certainly different than the dullness he felt on the plateau.

Then he looked up at the peak again and felt the same urge he had felt so many times before.

He wanted something better.

But he was not sure he was willing to climb up to the peak again. He might only be disappointed once more when he had to return to the valley.

That night, he slept poorly and wondered again if he should bother trying.

But he awoke the next morning thinking about the peak.

The more he thought about it, the more he wanted to return to the old man and ask him why the Peaks and Valleys approach had only worked for a little while.

Eventually, he left the plateau and returned to his valley. Over the next several days, he made plans to return to the peak.

This time, he hoped he would be better prepared for what the peak might hold for him.

5

Learning

The journey back up the mountain was difficult, and the young man was exhausted by the time he reached the peak. Still, he arrived in time to enjoy a beautiful sunset.

This time, he was invited to the old man's mountain home. He was surprised by its size and marveled at the superb craftsmanship.

Then the two men went out and sat on a huge deck overlooking a beautiful lake.

The young man said, "I can't tell you how happy I am to be back on this peak again."

The old man was pleased to see him, but saw he was troubled and asked why.

The young man said, "When I returned to my valley, I tried to use what you shared with me, like finding the good that is hidden in the bad time. It worked at first, but then things turned worse.

"I got discouraged, and went off to spend time on a plateau—but that didn't work so well."

"Was it a healthy or unhealthy experience for you?" the old man asked.

"I don't understand," the young man said.

The old man responded, "Have you ever seen something like this?"

The old man began to draw:

The young man said, "That looks like a tracing of a heartbeat."

"What do the ups and downs remind you of?"

"They look like Peaks and Valleys!"

"Yes. But what would this mean?"

This time he drew a straight line:

_____

The young man said, "I think that would mean that there is no heartbeat at all."

"Yes—a problem! Like a healthy heartbeat, your personal Peaks and Valleys are an essential part of a normal, healthy life.

"So are the Plateaus, if they are times of healthy rest when you take stock of what is happening and pause to think about what to do next.

"While it is unhealthy to try to escape by blocking out reality, it can often be very healthy to just relax and rest and trust that things will get better. Because, after a good night's sleep or a few days' break, they often do."

This time the young man had come prepared with a small notebook to record what he was discovering on the peak. He wrote:

A Plateau Can Be A Time
For You To Rest,
Reflect, And Renew.

The young man said, "My time on the plateau may have been unhealthy at first, but in the end it was good for me.

"I thought I had just given up when I went there. But afterward, I went back to my valley more rested and with a greater interest in coming back to this peak.

"Still," he wondered, "how can it be healthy to have ups and downs? How can that be peaceful? Don't all the highs and lows make you feel anxious and stressed out?"

The old man answered, "Only if you go up and down with them. Once you *truly* learn to manage your good and bad times, you gain a sense of healthy balance."

"But how?" the young man asked.

"To begin with, you become more peaceful once you realize that you are not your Peaks, your 'good' times, and you are not your Valleys, your 'bad' times.

"Then, you will no longer feel like you are on an emotional roller coaster."

The young man thought about that as they both looked quietly at the sunset.

Then the old man asked, "What happened when you first went back to your valley?"

The young man said, "The Peaks and Valleys approach seemed to be working for me. I had some real success at work. But then things went wrong, and I have no idea why."

The old man offered, "There was another reason I showed you the heart tracing. It was to encourage you to use the Peaks and Valleys approach with your *heart*."

"What do you mean?"

"It is not only the valuable insights you gain on the Peak that are important. It is also how you *feel* about the insights, and what you *do* with them that makes all the difference.

"For example, how do you behave when you are down in the valley?"

"How do I behave?" the young man asked.

"Yes. And when you returned to your valley, how did you feel?"

"I felt good. It was one good time!"

The old man said nothing.

"What?" the young man said, but the old man just waited. The young man realized what he had just said, and had a thought.

"Ohh . . . that's it, isn't it! The good time didn't last because of how I felt and what I did then."

The old man said, "Very good! Of course, it was not the good time itself, but how you did not manage things well during that good time. It may be helpful to think of it this way:

*You Can Have Fewer Bad Times
When You Appreciate And Manage
Your Good Times Wisely.*

The young man thought about this for a moment and said, "But I don't see what I did wrong. How did I manage my good times poorly?"

The old man said, "When you were feeling so good, did you perhaps boast a little about what you had discovered here on the peak?"

The young man said nothing.

"Do you think that may have happened?"

"I don't think so. Maybe."

The old man waited.

The young man sighed. "You know, that might explain why my friends have been avoiding me lately." He was thinking especially about the special young woman.

Then he said, "The first time I visited this peak, you said most people don't realize they need to be *truly* prepared if they want to stay on a Peak."

The old man smiled. "I'm glad you remember that. Those who are unprepared for a Peak soon fall from it, and they experience pain."

"How do you truly prepare to stay on a Peak?" asked the young man.

The old man said, "Instead of giving you *my* answers, perhaps I can help you find your *own* answers.

"When things started going wrong for you, how did you feel?"

"Awful," replied the young man.

"So why didn't you change your behavior?"

"I don't know," the young man admitted. "Maybe because I didn't know how to deal with it, or I thought if I just ignored it, things would somehow get better. Or maybe I was afraid to admit I'd been wrong, or that I needed help."

"And what would all these reasons have in common?" the old man asked.

The young man thought for a moment and said, "I'm not sure." He guessed, "Fear?"

The old man nodded. "Yes. And what is the source of a person's fear?"

The young man did not know.

"For most of us, it's ego," the old man said.

"Your ego can make you arrogant on the Peak, and fearful in the Valley. It keeps you from seeing what is real. Your ego distorts the truth.

"When you are on a Peak, your ego makes you see things as better than they really are. And when you are in a Valley, your ego makes you see things as worse than they really are.

"It makes you think a Peak will last forever, and it makes you fear a Valley will never end."

The young man wrote in his notebook what the old man went on to say:

The Most Common Reason
You Leave A Peak
Too Soon Is Arrogance,
Masquerading As Confidence.

The Most Common Reason
You Stay In A Valley
Too Long Is Fear,
Masquerading As Comfort.

The young man wanted to know, "How does arrogance take you off a Peak?"

The old man offered, "Let me give you an example. When I was younger, I worked for a very large and famous company. We provided a great service at a good price—the best in our industry.

"Then our costs rose and the economy took a turn for the worse. Our service cost us more to provide, and soon fewer people could afford it.

"Sales fell, but due to our fame, management believed they could simply ride out the bad time.

"The reality, of course, was that we needed to change. But they didn't see this, because their arrogance had made them complacent.

"Eventually we lost most of our customers and had to sell the business."

"So, what did *you* do?" the young man asked.

"I asked myself, *What is the truth in this situation?* The truth was that we were not making our customers happy.

"Then I began asking myself, *How can I be of more service?*

"Before long, I left and started my own company. I made that question the cornerstone of building my new business.

"Even though we started small, our customers had a great experience with us, and they told others. Over the years, we grew into a big company ourselves."

The young man asked what the name of his company was, and when the old man told him, he recognized it at once. He realized his new friend was a very wealthy man.

Apparently this Peaks and Valleys approach was really effective at work. But, he wondered, was it as useful in life?

He asked, "Can you tell me more about how it worked in your life?"

The old man thought for a moment, and then he said, "Yes. I'll share a personal example with you.

"When my wife became increasingly ill, it became a deeper and deeper Valley for us. She had always made raising our children, running our home, and nurturing all of us seem effortless.

"It was hard for us to see her in so much pain that she couldn't do the things she used to enjoy.

"I felt it was up to me to try to do much of what she once did. So, I struggled to take care of her and our children, help run the home, and continue with my work. Soon I was stressed out.

"Of course, what I was really worried about was her well-being. I didn't know what to do."

The old man's voice caught for a moment, as he remembered that dark time.

The young man said quietly, "That must have been very difficult."

"It was," the old man admitted. "I became afraid. I was worried about what would happen.

"I knew that fear can chase away truth. So I asked myself, *What is the truth of this situation?* And the truth was simple: *I loved her.*

"Then I asked myself, *What would be the most loving thing I could do right now?*

"At first I didn't know. But then I started doing whatever thoughtful things for her that I could think of. And soon, the situation didn't seem like such a deep Valley."

"Why was that?" the young man asked.

"Because I saw that my wife realized how much I loved her. It made her feel better. I knew I had not been as thoughtful before as I could have been. Soon, I enjoyed the feeling that comes with becoming a better person."

The old man added, "To my surprise, I began feeling more peaceful and successful, even in the terrible circumstances we found ourselves in.

"I realized that many of my fears were really about me, not about her. In looking for ways that I could be more loving, I shifted my focus from me to her. I managed to get outside myself."

"So," the young man realized, "when you put your *ego* aside, you are more likely to leave a Valley sooner."

"Exactly," the old man said. "And putting your ego aside can also help you stay on a Peak longer."

The young man thought about how important that was. He hoped he would remember it.

Later, he looked out into the distance and exclaimed, "Wow! Look at that."

The old man smiled. He knew the young man would see it sooner or later.

"Look at that great peak over there. It's even higher than this one," the young man said, as though the higher peak had just been discovered for the first time.

"I'll bet the view from there is even better than it is from here!"

"No doubt it is," the old man agreed.

"I've got to go see it," said the young man.

But then he looked down and saw the deep valley that lay between this peak and the higher peak. He groaned, knowing it might be hard to cross.

The old man asked, "When you look at that valley, what do you see?"

The young man thought for a moment and then laughed. "Pain?"

The old man laughed as well. "Many people see a deep valley that way. They see Valleys as times of frustration, hurt, disappointment, anger, and failure.

"But remember what happens when you find and focus on the good that is hidden there."

The young man nodded. "You can change a Valley into a Peak."

"Yes," the old man said. "But it takes a remarkable person to *truly* appreciate and use what lies hidden in a Valley. Do you think *you* can?"

The young man took a deep breath. "Thank you for reminding me of that. So, my challenge is to go through a Valley in a different way, isn't it? So, how do I do that?"

The old man said, "I find the best way to get through a Valley is by creating and following your own *sensible vision.*"

"What does that mean?"

"By *sensible,* I mean a vision of a future Peak you want to be on that makes good sense to you. Something as big as you can imagine that is also realistic and attainable if you want it enough.

"And *sensible* also means you can make what you imagine more real to you when you use all your five senses to create an image in such specific, believable detail that you begin to realize you can make it happen.

"Imagine how your future Peak will look, sound, smell, taste and feel, until it becomes so real to you that the image of getting there pulls you through your Valley."

The young man sensed how powerful this could be. He wrote:

*A Great Way To Get To Your Next Peak
Is To Follow Your Sensible Vision.*

*Imagine Yourself Enjoying Your
Better Future In Such Specific,
Believable Detail That You Soon
Enjoy Doing What Takes You There!*

The two men went on talking well into the evening.

Later that night, the young man went to his tent and dreamed about getting to a better place.

Early the next morning, he arose and gazed at the higher peak. Then he went to find the old man.

He said that he hoped it would not take too long to get to the next peak. He looked forward to an even greater view from up there once he arrived.

As they said their goodbyes, the old man made a suggestion.

"When you reach the higher peak, you might want to see if you can gain insights into deeper truths of your own.

"You might want to listen with your heart to your own thoughts, and recall real moments in your work and life that will guide you to your own truths.

"What you discover will become your *own* wisdom, not mine or anyone else's."

The young man said he would remember that, and he thanked the old man for sharing so much with him.

Then they shook hands, and the young man set off to cross the deep valley in his attempt to reach the higher peak beyond.

6

Discovering

The young man trudged along through the unfamiliar valley. Driving rain stung his face. He looked for shelter but found none.

The journey was proving to be even harder than he'd expected. When he set out, the valley had not looked *this* deep.

"Why does it have to be this way?" the young man muttered. "Aren't we supposed to be happy in life? Why do we need Valleys at all?"

His feet were soaked, and he felt chilled to the bone. He was miserable.

He said through clenched teeth, "One day I'll look back on this and laugh."

He thought about what he'd said, then added, "Why wait until later? Why not laugh at it now?"

He laughed out loud and felt a little better. Then his laughter was answered by a loud clap of thunder. He looked up anxiously, and hoped he would be safe from the lightning.

His legs ached and his feet hurt from walking over sharp rocks. He remembered the old man saying, *How you manage your Valley determines how soon you reach your next Peak.*

He didn't feel he was doing a very good job of managing this one.

Finally he reached the very lowest point of the valley and stopped.

The rain had completely washed away the path. Ahead, he saw nothing but a narrow, roaring river that seemed impossible to cross.

"I can't," he said aloud. "The current is too strong. I'll never make it."

He felt defeated.

He would have to turn around and go back the way he came. But how would he ever face the old man? How would he face himself?

The young man sat down in the mud and stared at the river. He feared he might wade into the river and be pulled under by the powerful current. He imagined swallowing mouthfuls of water as he went under and drowned.

He shuddered and asked himself, "Why does being in a Valley have to be so painful?"

And then he answered his own question by remembering something the old man had said:

The Pain In A Valley
Can Wake You Up
To A Truth
You Have Been Ignoring.

So, what truth was he ignoring?

He looked up at the higher peak in the distance.

"All I know," he thought, "is that I really wanted to be on that higher peak."

He wondered if there were a mountain lake up there that was as beautiful as the one in front of the old man's house—or even more so.

He wondered what the fresh air would feel like against his face.

Then he thought about what the old man had said about getting to your next Peak by creating and following a *sensible vision*—a picture of a better future that makes sense and that you draw on all five of your senses to imagine.

He realized that just moments ago, he had been creating a *fearful* vision—an image of himself drowning as he was being pulled into the river.

The old man had never talked about a "fearful vision," but that was exactly what the young man had been seeing.

"Maybe you are always creating a vision of your future," he thought, "whether you are aware of it or not—either a fearful vision, or a sensible vision. And it's just a question of which vision you follow."

And then he said, "Ohhh!—*that's it!*"

He spoke the words out loud into the rain and thunder around him:

My
Valley
IS
Fear.

He thought there were some kinds of Valleys—from illness or loss of a loved one, to financial reversals and other misfortunes—that might be beyond his control and were not caused by fear.

But more important, for him, he now also realized that he'd created many of his Valleys with his fear, whether he saw it at the time or not.

He wondered, since your Valleys are moments of longing for what is missing, did he fear that he would never gain or regain what was missing?

He knew the bad time can continue, but if you move beyond your fear, you soon feel much better.

After all, he was still soaking wet, sitting in the mud at the bottom of a valley, but he had to admit he felt better when he moved beyond his fear.

He knew he had often denied the reality that he might be responsible for some of his own Valleys.

He had certainly wished his Peaks would last longer. Now, looking at his work and life, it seemed like they had never lasted long enough. He also wished his Valleys would not go on so long.

Then he laughed. "I wish . . . I wish I had a wishing well. Maybe I could toss a few lucky coins into it and my wish to be on the other side of the river would come true."

He laughed again, and felt better, knowing that it's good to be able to laugh at yourself.

Then he remembered what the old man had been trying to tell him. He took out his pocket notebook and wrote:

*Avoid Believing Things Are
Better Than They Really Are
When You Are On A Peak,*

*Or Worse Than They Really Are
When You Are In A Valley.*

Make Reality Your Friend.

He looked at the peak again and imagined how it would feel to stand up there in triumph.

The old man had said that the most powerful tool to help you get through a Valley and arrive at your next Peak is to *follow a sensible vision*.

So, he began to create a sensible vision of his own. He closed his eyes and imagined, in realistic and believable detail, that he was already on the higher peak.

He saw the magnificent view. He felt the touch of the warm sun on him as he stood on the peak above the dark rain clouds. He tasted the water of the crystal clear lake. He smelled the tall pine trees and heard the cry of an eagle.

He was unaware of any fear. He felt peaceful.

He opened his eyes and looked back up at the peak, still imagining how good it would be to be up there. As he held on to his sensible vision, it seemed to pull him back up to his feet like a magnet.

He looked across the river at a tree stump on the other side. A plan formed in his mind.

He took out a rope from his backpack and made a lasso. Then he stood and threw it across the river. But it missed.

He threw it again many times, but the rope got wet and heavy, and became more difficult to toss.

He sank back to his knees, closed his eyes, and felt the throbbing pain in his arms and back.

He thought seriously about giving up.

But he looked at the higher peak again and recalled his sensible vision.

The young man looked across the river and focused on the tree stump as if nothing else existed. Still focusing, he threw the rope and this time it looped snugly over the stump. He pulled on it several times to make sure it was secure.

Then he entered the turbulent waters and slowly began pulling himself, hand over hand, to the far side.

Twice he was almost sucked under, but he hung on to the rope that he had secured on both sides of the river. It saved his life.

Eventually he reached the other side, and slowly clambered up the riverbank.

There he stood, raised both hands over his head, and yelled, "Yes!"

He laughed. Even though he was still down in the valley, he *felt* like he was up on the peak.

And all at once he understood what a personal Peak could be:

A Personal Peak
Is A Triumph
Over Fear.

He sat down and grinned. It felt great to have overcome his fear! He decided to rest for a while before setting out for the higher peak.

He wondered about the difference between wishing for a better future and following a sensible vision. Then he realized that the difference is in the *doing*.

"Wishing leads to no action," he thought. "But when you truly follow a sensible vision, you *want to do* the things that make it happen.

"You don't force yourself, you just *want to* so much that you find yourself doing things you never knew you were capable of."

He was beginning to understand what the old man meant by *truly* following your vision. It meant staying true to what you want and doing what really takes you there—recognizing the *truth*!

More and more, he was starting to realize that fear blocks you, but the truth helps you succeed.

He smiled and looked at the higher peak again. Soon he got up with renewed enthusiasm and continued his journey. He realized that once he had begun to follow his sensible vision, he had gained more energy and confidence.

As he climbed higher, he stepped on patches of loose rock and slid back down again. But each time, he resumed his climb.

He smiled as he made progress. He was on his way to a higher peak.

After what seemed like a long time, he emerged into the sunlight and stood atop the mountain.

He had come upon the most gorgeous lake, surrounded by great trees. He felt a fresh breeze.

Then he turned to look back at the valley he'd been through. He knew how difficult it had been. But it made things even sweeter now.

He thought about how things were back home in his own valley and recalled his old life and job.

He thought about his parents and friends and the young woman he cared about. He remembered how fearful he had been, although a lot of times he hadn't realized it.

He had been afraid his friends wouldn't like him. Afraid his father wouldn't respect him. Afraid the young woman he cared about would lose interest in him. Afraid he would lose his job. Afraid he would be viewed as a failure. He was probably afraid of other things, too.

He had been foolish to let fear run his life so often and cloud his view of the truth.

At last, he felt he really was beginning to live the Peaks and Valleys philosophy. He thought of it as "a philosophy with skills."

"It's a way of looking at things," he thought, "and just as important, it's a way of *doing* things."

Make reality your friend, the old man had said. He felt he was beginning to grasp what that could mean for him.

The pain he had felt in the Valley did indeed wake him up to some truths he had been ignoring.

He saw that when he not only faced the truth, but *embraced* the truth, it served him better.

Then he exclaimed, "That's why the old man uses the word 'truly' so often. He means based on *the truth!*"

He hoped he would now truly look for what was real, rather than live in illusion. He realized he could build a stronger foundation for the future if it was built on what was really true.

What amazed him most was the power of creating and following his sensible vision. As the old man had predicted, when he followed his sensible vision, he came up with surprising ways to make it happen.

He thought that following his sensible vision was like looking at a map. It was a practical way to help you get where you wanted to go.

The vision he had held of the peak had not only dissolved the fears that undermined him, but it had also given him the clarity and strength to go on.

"It's *truly* worth using again!" he said with a smile. And he wrote what he felt was an important entry in his notebook:

*You Create A Peak
When You Truly Follow
Your Sensible Vision.*

*Your Fear Fades And
You Become More
Peaceful And Successful.*

He sat quietly and listened to the whisper of wind in the trees on the peak and the gentle lapping of water at the lake's edge. It was as good as or even better than he had imagined it would be.

The young man felt a sense of freedom he had never felt before. He hoped he could share this feeling with those he cared about.

As he looked back toward his valley, he felt it would be good to get home again.

But before that, he wanted to spend time again with the old man. He began to imagine, in detail, what it would be like to be with the old man on his peak once more.

How lucky he was to have made changes in his life while he was still young! You didn't have to be old to gain wisdom, he realized.

Then, looking down over the valley, he spotted a shortcut he hadn't seen before.

He thought, "It's amazing how much more you can see from a higher point of view. I guess the key is, when you're in a Valley, to imagine seeing what you might see if you were on a Peak."

He liked the possibility of making discoveries in the Valley, so that his next Valley would be less painful, maybe even beneficial.

He planned to take the shortcut on his journey back to see the old man. "Now that I know a better way," he thought, "the time in the Valley will not be so painful."

He couldn't wait to see his old friend again.

7

Sharing

The young man reached the summit in the early afternoon. As soon as he saw the old man, he ran over and embraced him.

The old man laughed, "That's quite a greeting. I hardly recognized you! You don't look at all like the young fellow who turned up here that first evening. It is quite a journey, isn't it?"

"Yes it is," the young man said. "It took me a good deal longer than I thought it would to get to that higher peak."

"I meant, *life* is quite a journey."

"Ah," the young man said. "Yes, it certainly is."

Then he told him about what he had done since he'd left.

The old man asked, "So, what do you feel are the most important things you have discovered?"

"Well . . ." said the young man. "I've learned that it is not enough to simply know about Peaks and Valleys in your head, and talk about it—as I did when I went back to my valley the first time.

"You need to live the Peaks and Valleys philosophy. And the more you do, the more you learn and grow, and the more calm and successful you become.

"I've also learned that both the good and bad times in my life are truly gifts, and that each has great value, if I manage them well.

"When I was on my own up on the higher peak, I spent a lot of time looking at the truth, as best I could.

"Now I'm really looking forward to seeing my friends and family again. I realize I have so much I can learn from them, too."

The old man smiled. "I see that you've also learned something else."

"What do you mean?"

The old man said, "You've learned some *humility*. I'm glad you have, because now you are more likely to remain on your Peaks longer."

The young man just grinned.

The old man said, "Do you remember telling me when we first met how unhappy you felt living in your valley, and how nothing seemed to be working for you there?"

"Yes," the young man said, a little embarrassed. "That was because I did not appreciate that my Valley was an opportunity for me to grow—to create something better in my life. I was just trying to escape my Valley, not learn from it."

He added, "I see now that when I get outside myself and look for the gift hidden in that Valley, it can bring me to a new and better place."

The young man thought further and added, "I don't know if this is right, but it seems to me that the purpose of the Peak is to celebrate life, and the purpose of the Valley is to learn about life."

The old man smiled. "That's good. From the clarity in your eyes, I see you've discovered quite a bit about the truths of Peaks and Valleys."

The young man said, "You can see all that?"

The old man laughed. "It's not that hard to see!

"Tell me, what was it like when you reached the bottom of the valley? It is a very deep valley indeed."

The young man looked down for a moment, remembering what had happened.

"I came up against this roaring river that looked too dangerous to cross. I almost turned around and came back," he said.

"I feared I would fail. But then I remembered that it's our fear that keeps us trapped.

"More important, I discovered that I really *can* change a Valley into a Peak by letting go of my fear and getting outside of myself."

"How?" The old man was intrigued. "What did you do?"

"I remembered that a great way to get to my next Peak is to create and follow my *sensible vision*—one that makes *sense* to me and is realistic and attainable if I want it enough.

"I used all five of my senses to imagine that I was already enjoying being on the higher peak. I imagined what I would see, touch, taste, smell, and hear. As I did, my fear faded and it gave me the energy and enthusiasm to go for it.

"Then I kept seeing and feeling my sensible vision until I came up with a way to get there. I used my rope to lasso a tree stump on the other side and pulled myself across." He downplayed how difficult it had actually been.

"I got to the other side of the river and made my way up to the peak."

The old man asked, "What was the higher peak like?"

The young man's eyes sparkled. "It was . . . amazing!"

The old man laughed. "Amazing, how?"

The young man looked over at the higher peak in the distance. "It was breathtaking! I could see the valley I came through and I could see this peak."

He looked back at the old man.

"But the biggest thing I saw was why you use the word *truly* so often. Like *truly* appreciating and managing your good times and *truly* learning and making things better in your bad times.

"You mean seeing *the truth*! Not what I wish for, or fear is happening, but what is really true about my good or bad time.

"Now I'm hoping that I can experience my future Peaks and Valleys with more curiosity about the truth. I'll ask myself, *What is the truth in this situation I'm in?*"

The old man said, "I just got 'truth bumps,' what most people call 'goose bumps.' It happens when I hear a truth."

The young man laughed and thanked the old man. They continued on talking until it was time for the young man to return to his valley home.

When they said their good-byes, they did not know it would be the last time that they would see each other.

8

Using Peaks And Valleys

When the young man returned to his valley, his family and friends noticed that he had changed a great deal. They enjoyed being around him more, although they did not know why.

However, the company was in trouble and losing even more money.

The young man thought back to the days when he first joined the prosperous company, and he wondered why things were so different now.

He remembered when they used to feel excited about looking for ways to improve every aspect of the business. They often asked themselves questions, and did not assume they already knew the answers. They took nothing for granted.

But success had gone to their heads. They were not doing the things that had made them successful. They'd lost that sense of urgency and curiosity.

Instead, as things turned bad, many became anxious or even angry. When they tried to fix things, their energy went in the wrong directions, blaming others or defending themselves.

No wonder the company couldn't seem to get out of its Valley. Too many employees' thoughts and actions were actually deepening and extending the Valley.

Then one day at work, the company was hit with what everyone thought was very bad news.

They had been the exclusive manufacturer of a unique and very profitable product. Now, a much bigger company was entering their field and coming out with a similar product at a lower price.

With its huge marketing budget, the bigger company might easily put them out of business.

His company created a new marketing plan, but people had little hope that it would do much good.

The young man met with his department and asked everyone to think about two questions:

What is the truth in this situation? How can we use the good that's hidden in this bad time?

He encouraged everyone to offer their best answers in an emergency meeting scheduled for early the next morning.

When the meeting began, one woman said, "No one knows more about this kind of product than we do. We have more customers who have been using this product longer than anyone else."

Someone added: "The truth is they have a huge marketing budget. We need to do something we are better at than they are."

The team agreed that both things were true.

Then the young man asked, "So where is the hidden good in this bad time that we can use to our advantage?"

One older gentleman said, "What if we focus on staying ahead of our competition by coming up with a much better product than theirs?"

Suddenly the young man's team saw the hidden good: The competitor's big marketing campaign would make people more aware of this kind of product—but *they* would have the better product.

In a way, their competitor would be doing their marketing for them!

The young man asked the team if they wanted to create and follow a *sensible vision*—a picture of a better future that made sense to them.

The team agreed and began to imagine, in specific and believable detail, what it would be like to have a far better product—one that customers loved so much they would buy it, use it, *and* tell others about it.

The team imagined listening to customers to learn what they *truly* wanted, and sharing what they learned with the rest of the company.

Then they *did* it! They listened and added wonderful features to their product that people valued. By the time their giant competitor's marketing began, their own company had improved the product greatly, and many more customers bought it.

They gained a reputation for great service, and as word spread, the company's fortunes rose.

People's jobs soon became more secure.

The young man went on to share more of what he had learned about Peaks and Valleys with others in the company.

They discussed it among themselves and realized their former arrogance had taken them off their Peak, and vowed they would not become so complacent again.

The young man and his team received a raise, and they continued to look for new ways to help the company. They asked questions and did not assume that they knew all the answers.

The young man was happy to see his company back on a Peak again, but he also knew how easy it would be to fall into a Valley if they didn't manage this good time wisely.

He remembered what he had learned:

To stay on a Peak longer: Be humble and grateful. Do more of what got you there. Keep making things better. Do more for others. Save resources for your upcoming Valleys.

He smiled, knowing that he was finally learning how to manage his good times better.

He had already decided he would do things differently in the future, including saving and investing some of his increased salary to help him through the Valleys that would surely come his way.

One day, the young man was surprised and happy to learn that he had been promoted!

He could not wait to share his news with his family and the young woman he cared about.

And then, his heart sank.

The last time he had shared great news from work, it had not gone well.

He recalled, when he began to succeed before, how arrogant he had been and how unaware of it he was.

He remembered how his friends had begun avoiding him, including the young woman he cared about.

Now he was afraid that his boastful ways might have cost him his relationship with her.

But instead of becoming discouraged by his fear, he resolved to apply his new Peaks and Valleys approach. He would say less and do more.

"If I do lose this relationship," he told himself, "I will trust that there is a hidden good in that Valley, too.

"Or better yet, maybe I can create a better relationship with her when I have learned to be a little more humble and a lot more loving."

Then he laughed at himself. "A *little* more humble?" he said out loud.

He decided he wanted to grow into a more loving and attractive person.

He now believed that by becoming more loving himself—by replacing fear with love—he was more likely to *be* loved, and to attract a truly fulfilling relationship into his life.

In the days that followed, he created another *sensible vision*. This time, he imagined himself becoming the kind of person that a woman like her would want to be with. And perhaps more important, the kind of person he would like to *be*.

He imagined his better self in every detail. He would become someone who didn't take himself too seriously, someone who was fun to be with, yet someone who cared deeply about creating real excellence in his life and work.

He would be a man who wanted to make a difference in the world—perhaps a small difference, but a significant one. And he would never take for granted the people closest to him.

For a change, the young man did not talk about this to anyone. He just held this picture and feeling very clearly in his mind and heart.

Then he *did* the things that made it happen—starting with small things. In time, he became more like the man he had imagined.

He remembered asking long ago, *Exactly how do you manage a Valley?*

Now he wrote his answer in his notebook:

*You Get Out Of A Valley Sooner
When You Manage To Get
Outside Of Yourself:*

*At Work, By Being Of
Greater Service,*

*And In Life, By Being
More Loving.*

One evening, before he started to work in his new position, his parents held a small celebration for him. Most of his friends came, including the young woman who had now grown fond of him.

Late that night, he asked his father what his life had been like as a young man. As he listened to his father's stories about some of the personal Peaks and Valleys he'd had on his own journey, he realized that his father had a wisdom of his own.

Over time, the two men began to grow closer.

The young man's career continued to flourish and his parents were happy for him.

He still argued with them at times, but he had become less defensive and their arguments were mild. Many turned into thoughtful discussions.

The young man went on to make many discoveries of his own. One of the most useful things he found was surprisingly simple: Whenever he got confused about how to get out of a Valley, he remembered that Peaks and Valleys are opposites. So, he looked at what he did that put him in the Valley, and then he did just the opposite—and he got the opposite results!

It was amazing how obvious this was, but he couldn't get over how well it worked.

As he grew older, he began to pass through his Valleys with increasing grace and serenity.

Despite his busy schedule, the young man still made time to walk in his valley's meadows—often with the young woman he cared about.

Then one day, he received painful news he knew would come sooner or later. The old man of the peak had died.

All who had known him said they could feel his presence, especially near the summit. Even after he was gone for a long time, his friend from the valley knew he would miss him very much.

The young man looked out at the valley. He feared an important part of his life was now missing and would be gone forever. He had grown very attached to the old man, and now he began to feel more alone and unhappy.

He felt the pain in his heart, and wondered what the truth was.

Then he imagined the old man's voice, saying, *A Valley is a time when you long for what is missing . . .*

And then he laughed, and in a whisper finished the old man's sentence:

"And a Peak is a time when you appreciate what you have."

He thought about what he had to appreciate.

The truth was that he now had a way of working and living that clearly made him more peaceful and successful in both good and bad times.

And he had gotten that from his old friend.

He knew he had been in a personal Valley just moments ago, because he thought the old man should still be with him, sharing his wisdom and his zest for life.

But now, the young man took a deep breath, and looked at what was *real*—not at what he wished for or feared was real.

The truth was the old man had given him gifts that, if he applied them, would serve him and those around him well for many years to come.

In a way, part of the old man was *within* him, and would always be with him.

His eyes moistened. He felt the sadness and joy of having had such a good friend in his life.

He realized that his work and life would always be a series of Peaks and Valleys.

He would live through times of financial, emotional, and spiritual ups and downs; through health and illness, joy and pain.

He accepted that this repeating pattern was part of the complex richness of being alive.

But now he knew that using the Peaks and Valleys approach could really help make the good and bad times work better for him.

He thought about how much his work and life had changed, and how grateful he was to his old friend. Then he remembered the promise he had made the day they first met.

"I'll tell you about Peaks and Valleys," the old man had said, "on the same condition my friend asked of me—that is, if you find it useful, you'll see if you can find a way to share it with others."

The young man thought he had tried to do that the best he could. But now he felt he wanted to do more. He wanted to find a better way to share the gifts his old friend had given him.

So, he went down by the river to a friend's cabin where he could be alone and think.

He asked himself what he had found most useful about the Peaks and Valleys approach. He thought about his own experiences. And he looked back through the notes he had taken. There were so many things that he found helpful.

Eventually he began to write a summary of what he found most valuable. He made it brief so it could fit on a small card.

He planned to share it with those who really wanted to know.

Then he smiled, as he realized the card could be a useful reminder for *him*, too. It could help him remember to use the remarkable Peaks and Valleys principles and tools more often.

In the days and months that followed, he found several opportunities to help others by passing along the summary.

Using Your Peaks and Valleys
At Work and In Life

To Manage Your Good and Bad Times:
Make Reality Your Friend

Whether you are temporarily up on a Peak or down in a Valley, ask yourself: *What is the truth in this situation?*

To Get Out Of A Valley Sooner:
Find And Use The Good Hidden In A Bad Time

Relax, knowing that Valleys end. Do the opposite of what put you in the Valley. Get outside of yourself: be of more service at work and more loving in life. Avoid comparisons. Uncover the good that is hidden in a bad time, and use it soon to your advantage.

To Stay On A Peak Longer:
Appreciate and Manage Your Good Times Wisely

Be humble and grateful. Do more of what got you there. Keep making things better. Do more for others. Save resources for your upcoming Valleys.

To Get To Your Next Peak:
Follow Your Sensible Vision

Imagine yourself enjoying a better future in such specific, believable detail, that you soon enjoy *doing* what takes you there.

To Help People:
Share It With Others!

Help people make good and bad times work for them, too.

9

Enjoying A Peak

Many decades later, the once-young man had grown into an old man himself.

He had moved long ago to his own peak where he lived most of the time, although he still returned occasionally to the valley.

One day after lunch, he sat under a tree, enjoying the magnificent view.

He thought back on his life and recalled how, when he was younger, he had created many of his good and bad times without realizing it.

He fondly remembered the old man who had shared with him such invaluable ways to deal with the ups and downs that came his way.

What an extraordinary difference it had made in his work and life. He had become remarkably peaceful and successful in both good and bad times.

He remembered how much he owed the old man.

Then, he smiled as he imagined the old man's voice reminding him that the real credit goes to the person who learns and *uses* it.

Then he heard a sound and turned to look.

But he did not see anything and returned to his thoughts.

He valued the time when he had been back in his valley. But he preferred to spend most of his time on the higher peak, where he had built a great home.

He enjoyed inviting friends and family here to join him. He earned a reputation as a generous host and thoughtful friend.

And he had been happily married for many years now, to that special woman who had grown to love him dearly.

The man realized that what counted was not where a person lived, but *how* a person lived.

It did not matter whether it was in a fertile valley like his parents, or on a magnificent peak like the old man.

Now he lived what he knew: that a joyful, rich life is a naturally changing landscape of Peaks and Valleys. At last, he felt that he was not only on a peaceful journey, but that even before he reached his destination, he had already arrived.

He smiled.

The sound he thought he had heard earlier grew louder and nearer.

He looked up and saw a startled young woman, who said, "Sorry. I didn't mean to intrude on you."

She explained that she had just come up to the peak after a long journey from her valley home. She looked like she was more than tired.

As they began to talk, she was surprised to hear herself describing to a total stranger some of the difficulties she was having in her valley.

For reasons she did not understand, the young woman felt there was something special about this old man. At that moment, the young woman had no way of knowing that she was meeting one of the most peaceful and successful people in the world. He just seemed like a nice old man.

As the day went on, they began to discuss what the old man called a Peaks and Valleys approach. He said it was a philosophy with skills—a way of looking at things and doing things that makes you calmer and more successful in good and bad times.

He noticed she listened well and hoped she would use what she was about to discover at an even younger age that he did.

He thought, *It's never too soon to make good and bad times work for you.*

When she asked to know more, the old man readily agreed, on one condition.

The young woman quickly responded, "Yes. If I find it works as well for me as it seems to have worked for you, I would be honored to . . .

Share It With Others

the end

After The Story

As Ann finished the story, Michael nodded. He seemed to be lost in thought.

Eventually he said, "You've given me a lot to think about. I guess I'm actually wondering how I could apply this story in real life. My situation is complicated."

Ann nodded. "That's how I felt when I first heard the story. Until it occurred to me that maybe I was the one complicating things."

"How so?" Michael asked.

"The more I thought about the story, the more it seemed like . . . well, great common sense."

Michael sipped his coffee slowly and said, "There is a lot to this." Then he paused and added, "I hope I can remember to use it."

Ann reached into her purse and handed him a small card. She offered, "Here, this may help."

Michael saw that it was a summary of the Peaks and Valleys approach to managing good and bad times. He said, "Thank you very much!"

Ann smiled. "My pleasure. Besides, I promised the person who first told me that when I had the opportunity, I would—"

"Share it with others?" Michael said.

Ann laughed. "How did you guess?"

For the next few days Michael wondered how he might use what he got from the story to solve some real problems he was having.

The software company where Michael worked had begun sending many of its jobs overseas. He had the feeling his job might be next.

What is the hidden good in this bad time? He couldn't really see anything good about it.

What is the truth in this situation? The truth was, he was good at what he did. But another truth was that the market for what he did was evaporating. Or was it?

Be of more service. How did that apply here?

Peaks and Valleys are connected. The wise things you do in today's Valleys create tomorrow's Peaks.

Was his company clinging to the past? Perhaps they needed to take a fresh look at how they might service new types of clients.

Maybe now was the time to start envisioning their next peak—in thorough, realistic detail.

He started sharing this thought with a few people at work who seemed open to new ideas.

They formed a working group and found several innovative ways to provide better service to more clients. When they *did* the things that made it happen, it made a big difference!

And the more they did, the more things improved.

As things began looking up at work, Michael's thoughts turned to home.

Things with his wife, Linda, were not great. The stress of both their jobs and their difficult financial times had been hard on their marriage.

Michael remembered how happy he and Linda had been when they were first married.

Do more of what got you there.

What had taken them to that happy place? What did they need to do more of again?

He remembered how he used to notice so many things about Linda that he loved and appreciated. Now, had he taken these things for granted?

He looked for ways to get outside himself and be more loving. He started doing little things for her. It didn't take long for Linda to notice.

Later, he told her about the Peaks and Valleys story and the impact it had on him.

"Things have really improved between us," he said. He paused.

Linda finished his thought. "That's true. But you're still in a deep Valley with Kevin."

Michael nodded. He and their teenage son were on such bad terms, they were hardly speaking.

He wished Kevin would take his academics more seriously, and not spend so much time playing music with his friends.

He had been thinking about this for days, asking himself, *What is the truth in this situation?*

The truth was that he didn't like his son's interest in music, but the boy *loved* it.

Wishing leads to no action. Michael knew he had to stop wishing and *make reality his friend.*

He decided to create a sensible vision for the two of them. He imagined what kind of father he wanted to be and what kind of friendship he wanted to have with his son. He couldn't control what his son did, but he could control what *he* did.

He imagined going to hear a concert, with Kevin's band performing—the sound of the audience cheering and clapping, the look of joy and pride on Kevin's face. The feeling of his son giving him a bear hug backstage after the concert.

And then he began to *do* the things that would take him to the Peak he had created in his mind.

He stopped criticizing his son, and began going down to the basement to listen when the boy's band met to practice. He didn't say anything. He just listened, smiled, and waved when he left.

It didn't happen quickly, but over time Kevin began responding to his dad's change of heart.

Linda couldn't help but notice and asked, "What's happening to my former cynic?"

Michael laughed.

Linda began wondering if there might be some way she could use the Peaks and Valleys approach in her own work.

The school where she worked had just gone through another budget cut, and times were tense.

One day, she shared the Peaks and Valleys story with a friend on the faculty, who had an idea: Why not teach this approach to the students?

The two of them began setting up Peaks and Valleys study groups, and meeting with students after school to help them deal with their hard times and get the most out of their good times.

Soon the Peaks and Valleys approach was having an impact on a lot of kids' lives—and on the teachers' lives, too. It spread to other schools, and Linda was put in charge of the program.

Linda loved telling Michael about it. One evening, they celebrated by going out to dinner at the same small café where Michael had first heard about Peaks and Valleys from Ann Carr.

They both knew that their work and lives had improved, but they were realistic enough to realize that there might well be some bad times ahead.

However, they also knew that they now had some remarkable principles and practical ways to help them make their good and bad times work better for them.

And they felt very good knowing that they would have many other opportunities to share it with others.

About The Author

Spencer Johnson, M.D., is one of the world's most respected thinkers and beloved authors.

His eleven international bestselling books include the No. 1 titles *Who Moved My Cheese?®An A-Mazing Way to Deal with Change,* the most widely read book on change, and *The One Minute Manager,*® the world's most popular management method for more than two decades, coauthored with Kenneth Blanchard.

Dr. Johnson is often referred to as "the best there is at taking complex subjects and presenting simple solutions that work."

He received a B.A. degree in psychology from the University of Southern California, an M.D. degree from the Royal College of Surgeons, and completed medical clerkships at the Mayo Clinic and the Harvard Medical School.

He has served as Leadership Fellow at the Harvard Business School, and is currently Advisor to the Center for Public Leadership at Harvard's John F. Kennedy School of Government.

His work has captured the attention of major media, including the Associated Press, the BBC, CNN, *Fortune,* the *New York Times,* the *Today* show, *Time* magazine, *USA Today,* and United Press International.

More than forty-six million copies of Spencer Johnson's books are in print worldwide in more than forty-seven languages.